SEVEN GATEWAYS TO HAPPINESS

Freeing Your Enchanted Self

By

Dr. Barbara Becker Holstein

Enchanted Self Press

Long Branch, NJ

USA

Dr. Barbara Becker Holstein, internationally known Positive Psychologist, is the creator of The Enchanted Self®, a systematic way of helping bring more joy, meaning, and purpose into our lives.

Dr. Holstein has been a school psychologist for over 25 years. She also taught first and second grades. She is in private practice as a psychologist, with her husband, Dr. Russell M. Holstein, for over 25 years, in Long Branch, New Jersey.

You can find Dr. Holstein on the web at **www.enchantedself.com** *and write to her at* **drbarbara@enchantedself.com**.

Blogs: **www.thetruthforgirls.com**
www.next-year-in-jerusalem.com

SEVEN GATEWAYS TO HAPPINESS
Freeing Your Enchanted Self

You are about to embark on a wonderful adventure!

I've been a positive psychologist in private practice for twenty-five years. I've been a school psychologist for over twenty-five years and a researcher of women in and out of my practice. I have some important news to share about happiness and about how women can be happy.

I have discovered some things about us women. Here are some of the relevant truths:

1. When we fly, we don't fly like crows. We fly in circles. Yet we can hone in like the greatest of the homing pigeons!

2. We have an ENCHANTED SELF-a place inside of ourselves where we can feel peace of mind, a sense of well-being and we can mobilize for action using our best talents, strengths and even lost potential.

3. We diminish and disregard our Enchanted Selves and often are influenced by other factors and persuasive circumstances that keep us from feeling good, fulfilling our dreams and even remembering what those dreams are!

4. We are not knowledgeable in how to read our own selves so as to help ourselves recognize what is most unique about ourselves, what is most central to our beings and what is right for our health in mind, body and spirit.

5. We haven't had a good framework around which to sort through the complexities and distractions that come into our lives, pushing us from our Enchanted Selves.

6. The good news is we can come home to our Enchanted Selves.

7. The Seven Gateways to Happiness is our
    roadmap back to our Enchanted Selves.

How did I discover the Enchanted Self and what is it?
I discovered the Enchanted Self searching for the
origins of pain and dysfunction that I saw in my
clients, my friends, my family and myself. I was
searching in particular for how women lived with,
and handled dysfunctional or hurtful or painful
messages we absorb along the way, whether in
childhood or later. I wanted to see what these insults,
these violations, and these hurts did to us. For
instance, what was the result emotionally for my
patient when she had a great idea and was told by her
husband, "That and 5 cents will get you a cup of
coffee". Another example, what were the emotional
results of being told as a young teen that you are
dumb but beautiful? That you have a choice of being
either a secretary or a saleslady?

To research I decided to interview women not in my
practice. I did case study interviews on eighteen

3

women, ranging in age from 35 until the early 80's. I found each had hurt feelings and/or weakened self-esteem at some point growing up or in a marriage. However, my research yielded far more information that I had not expected.

In fact, I had a profound "aha" experience as I reviewed the transcriptions of my interviews. I saw that each woman had a capacity for joy, for elation, a sense of well-being, and all had ways of making their lives special and meaningful. They had fun. They enjoyed much of their daily lives. They had stories to tell of successes, both personal and professional. All of their wonderful capacities were much more than I anticipated.

I was elated, yet confused. The equation was not equal. Although hurt by negative experiences in their lives, all of the women still were to experience in some measure, pleasure, happiness, a sense of fulfillment, humor, fun, exuberance with others, etc.

There was no way that one could fully explain where these capacities could come from or how the women were able to always harness them. However, what I did discover is that these women that often they did not know how to talk about their capacities, tended to diminish them as quickly as they were brought up and they were not necessarily framing them within a context of a personal talents or potential or even strengths or coping skills.

As a psychologist, I well knew how powerful memory can be. I began to wonder, what if I could help women link to their most positive memories more often. What if we could really explore in the treatment room what was right about ourselves and the story of our lives, by the ways we access memory, rather than looking for what went wrong? What if we explored the positive parts of us that we had experienced earlier in life? What if we took the time to search for our lost potential even if it had been thwarted?

I had a hunch that all of us could learn how to sift through old memories for good news. I began to develop techniques to help women do this retrieval work. I became excited and so did the women, as we all became pathfinders in our own behalf, searching for our talents, strengths, and lost potential. Often this search became very important, as the woman would now have the chance to become the person she was meant to be!

It became clear that what I was beginning to call The Enchanted Self was the core part of each woman. It was in the past, in the present and would be there for our futures. But we had to learn how to fly. The strengths, talents and potential had to be reclaimed and reframed for the present and the future. Each woman has to learn to recognize what is best for her, whether finding a way to earn a living, relate to a mate or know what made her really happy.

Helping my clients retrieve themselves from their past in positive terms was a big step forward. Still, was it enough? Did it open the doors to enough growth, pleasure and purpose? I began to see over the years that even an Enchanted Self capacity to recognize what gives us pleasure, what works for ourselves and to have some sense of self-appreciation around these capacities is not necessarily enough.

We as women often times are like the very central characters of those fairytales we knew so well at a very early stage in our lives. Some of us repeat the saga of Sleeping Beauty. We are imprisoned by repetitive conditions that inhibit the real flowering of our true selves. We either are engaged in repetitive negative relationships that don't serve us well or live in circumstances that constantly keep us down or have dreams that are so unattainable that there is a sense of failure and feeling so bad about ourselves that we are not able to be in tune with our own energies and move forward.

For some of us, we are more like Cinderella. We not only wait for Prince Charming but we are often in situations where we are taken for granted where we don't get our fair share, where there is some manipulation going on to undermine or hurt and we become convinced along with the perpetrators that we are less than we can be. Sometimes we are lucky and we get to the ball and we meet the prince. But, sometimes we can't handle the prince. It is just too much, too good, too fast. So, sometimes we let the carriage turn into the pumpkin.

Some of us are very much like The Princess and The Pea. We feel everything exquisitely.
We are so sensitive that we could be used in scientific tests to measure the absorption of one tiny remark on the human body system but the sensitivity doesn't fill us well. It ends up keeping us up at night, keeping us from not getting where we should go because we are always feeling violated or talked about or criticized or not appreciated.

How do we get this fabulous, intact woman that we each have inside of ourselves to emerge?

Helping Your Enchanted Self Emerge

It is very helpful to have a plan, a kind of model to keep us on track as we grow and flower. Certainly not a clinical model that may make us feel there is something wrong with us.

That's where the Seven Gateways to Happiness come in. There are Seven Gateways to walk through. To obtain true happiness we must go through all the Gateways at one time or another in your life. You will recognize all of them as essential parts of being alive.

The Seven Gateways to Happiness are in an order that goes from where we often have to start as women and finishes where we long to be as competent adults. Yet, it is also a structure that can be varied and changed as suits each woman's needs. You may even find yourself in two or three Gateways at once or see that once you start in one Gateway in order to continue growing you must tap into another.

Welcome to the complexity of being a marvelous woman!

The Seven Gateways to Happiness:

The First Gateway is the self-esteem gateway. It is the Gateway where we come to value our thoughts, our talents, our memories, our potential, and our feelings about our purpose in life, our coping skills, our dreams, and our desires.

The Second Gateway is at the emotional gut level. It is falling in love with ourselves, which means seeing ourselves as a heroine, within the framework of our own lives. It is a way of giving dignity and purpose to our lives regardless of what flaws or mistakes have happened.

The Third Gateway is the gateway of learning how to meet our needs and negotiate for ourselves and how to facilitate a life. It is a gateway that often no one bothers to teach women. Often we don't know how to ask for a raise or share feelings with our husbands or how to negotiate space with a mother-in-law. These are all communication skills that involve ways of speaking and ways of behaving that can be challenging. Other stressors such as medical care, more education, relocation, are also challenges that involve facilitating a life. .

The Fourth Gateway is the gateway of pleasure and rejuvenation. It is the gateway of joy. It is where we learn how we have a right to take care of ourselves and also a right to feel pleasure, to feel joyful, to be the one to put on the oxygen mask first and feel comfortable with that decision. It is the Gateway where we feel entitled to get a kick out of life This gateway may have to be partnered with a husband or a partner and we thrust into issues of negotiation. So you begin to see that the gates overlap each other.

The Fifth Gateway is the gate of belonging. This gate keeps us from becoming isolated and depressed. We need company; we need to feel connected and wanted by other people. Often when we are so down on ourselves we pull back. So, finding the right people, having the courage to stay connected to them, working on one's self-esteem even when we are not feeling great, all of this is work. The results are good mental health and a full life. I think the results are worth it.

The Sixth Gateway, which is the gateway of mentoring and wisdom. It is the gateway that women often shortchange. We are shy and hesitant to ask for help. Often we don't know how to find the right mentors, nor do we realize the tremendous wisdom and knowledge that we already have and that we can pass on to others. This is the Gateway where women learn to mentor and be mentored and to create shared wisdom that can be passed down generationally. .

The Seventh Gateway is the Gateway of positive action and good deeds. This Gateway bridges into the spiritual. Here we make sense of a life worth living, as we live with purpose and dignity, helping others as well as ourselves. Here is the Gateway we can always fall back on, even when our mood or events may keep us from the experience of happiness. All through history, we have known the benefit of a good deed and helping others. Research also validates that the giver benefits emotionally from giving. So soon you will be back on the road to happiness!

Let's take some time to go through each Gateway now. I encourage you to do the exercise that follows each Gateway.

First Gateway: Honoring what is Right about Ourselves
Rather Than What is Wrong

As women, we're all experts in identifying what is wrong with ourselves. We can probably quickly make up a long list, detailing what is wrong in our lives. However, it's a lot harder to get in touch with what is right.

We need to know ourselves in positive ways. We need to learn how to honor our talents, strengths, even our coping skills, which serve us so well. And most important, we need to treasure and enjoy our potential.

These parts of us, if not honored, identified and talked about both to ourselves and to others, will lose their power. We have to ignite them and nurture their specialness. We need to get to know ourselves in ways that emphasize the heroic, strong parts of ourselves.

This means using our memories in very different

ways from what we've been accustomed to. It means searching through our history to find our talents, strengths and even lost potential, even if we have to sort through pounds of dysfunction. It means searching our past for what is right about ourselves, not for what is wrong.

Case Vignette

Stacie had very negative feelings toward her mother and her aunt, who would both often put her down and criticize her. However, once she was well into her therapy, she began to enjoy sorting through her past, realizing that many of the talents and strengths she had acquired had been based either by example from these women, or by compensating for their deficits. By example, she had learned to sew, cook and have the best vegetable garden that anyone could imagine, even while working full time. By compensating, she learned to guard her tongue and never jump to criticize others. This latter capacity has served her well in her job, while the former gave her day-to-day pleasure in hobbies and in good food.

A Positive Activity for You

Pick a time period from earliest childhood to the
present. Find a quiet spot, a quiet time, and begin to
list the talents, strengths, coping skills and potential
that you got and currently display from that time
period. You may have to sort through
disappointments and hurts, but you will still find a
way to label what's right about yourself.

Take your time. Keep this list with you, and add to it
over the next few weeks or even months. Read it
again and again to reinforce within you what is right
within you, rather than what is wrong.

Take a moment to think about this gateway before
you go on to the next.

Gateway Two: Falling in Love with Ourselves

This is an extremely important gateway. This gateway is achieved after we have made efforts to reclaim and honor our talents, capacities, strengths, lost potential and coping skills.

Now we are ready. We no longer break our hearts by putting ourselves down and saying "No, no, you can't do that," or "You're stupid." Now we are ready to say, "Yes, I love myself. I have a lot to offer. I am capable of having fun. I am capable of doing good, and no one can sidetrack me from who I really am."

When you fall in love with yourself, you begin to feel the positive self-esteem that comes when we don't deflate ourselves. You're ready to take yourself out for tea or to that wonderful spa for a day, or to go back and play the piano, which you always wanted to do. You're ready to recognize all the tools of wisdom that you have to offer. You're ready to recognize that you have an Enchanted Self that deserves to be part of your every day.

When you love yourself, you know when you need help. You know when you need guidance. It isn't a narcissistic love where you feel that you are perfect. It's a love of yourself, as you would love a child. If the child is ill, you take the child to the doctor. If the child comes home with a good paper from school, you put it on the refrigerator. It's a self-acknowledgment that makes you viable, real, and whole. Now you've become really ready to see the story of your life in a positive light. Even the disappointments, even tragedies have served only to hone you like tempered steel. You've been through the battles and have emerged stronger. You're in charge of your own self, a most wonderful feeling!

Case Vignette

Charlotte was constantly demeaned and criticized by her husband. Once she fell in love with herself, she had the courage to no longer put up with his attacks.

When he became verbally abusive, she left the house and indicated that if he was not in a better mood and could not behave more appropriately when she returned home, she would leave for good.

Her husband slowly mended his ways and became less verbally inappropriate as time went on. And because Charlotte had learned to love herself, she found that she was able to do what she needed to do for herself. This included becoming more independent and spending time away from her husband.

Perhaps another woman would have left, but for her it made sense to build a world that still included him, but also included her own time for herself - for sports, spas, individual time with her grandchildren, time to enjoy music, time alone with women friends.

Although she stayed, she had become strong. Her love of herself made her conceivably able to leave at any point in time if she was not treated appropriately.

Her husband realized this, and did not test the waters too deeply. A satisfactory conclusion had been reached, due to Charlotte's "new" self.

Positive Activity for You

Think about the story of your life. Think about it in positive terms where every hurdle ultimately resulted in some wisdom or in a turn in the road, which had some good in it. Start to tell the story of your life to yourself, making yourself the heroine, and remember to make yourself a lovable heroine. You may find yourself going over the same material that we've talked about before, merely giving it a different twist to more clearly identify your talents, strengths and potential. Enjoy the positive story of your life. Discover how special you really are.

Take a moment to think about this gateway before you go on to the next.

Gateway Three: Learning to Meet Our Needs and Negotiate Successfully

There's nothing more demoralizing than a woman who does not know how to speak up for herself, who doesn't have a voice for herself. When we feel ignored or not understood, we can feel rage and anger building.

So often as women we find ourselves in a predicament where we don't know how to speak up. We simply don't know how to negotiate for what we want. While sometimes it's a cultural attitude that we've taken on, for instance that women should be demure, quiet, and modest, often it's due to a lack of understanding the appropriate skill-set necessary for negotiating effectively. All of these factors put a tremendous pressure on our true capacities. Our future happiness or fulfillment is restricted simply because we don't know the right road to get there.

Learning how to meet our needs and how to negotiate appropriately is a lot of work, but the satisfaction far outweighs the work. When you have been able to speak with integrity to a husband, mother-in-law or a boss, when you have been able to finish a level of training that moves you ahead professionally; you're really living your Enchanted Self. You feel as special as you deserve to feel. It's worth every moment of effort.

Case Vignette

Deborah had been hiding the bookshelves under her side of the bed for so long, she couldn't remember how many years they had been there.

Why were they under the bed? Because when she had brought them home, pretty and ornate with fancy wrought iron underpinnings, her husband had belittled the purchase and belittled her. "Those were stupid purchases," he had said. "They're too ornate. They're flimsy. They'll fall off the wall. You don't even know how to put them up. And don't think I'll help you." Finishing his tirade, he had turned around and stormed out of the room.

Deborah felt devastated. Not only had she believed they were perfect for the family room, but they had reminded her of some lovely built-in mahogany shelving that her grandmother used to have. But apparently that was then and this was now. It obviously didn't fit into "now." Her husband had just told her so.

Back in therapy, Deborah confronted once again some of the pain and inertia she had been living with, as well as the pain that was a result of the negative interactions that had continued between her husband and herself. She was determined to move ahead emotionally and to finally gain some resiliency.

While she wasn't ready to leave her husband, she was ready to put up those shelves. One day she took them out from under her side of the bed, brought them into the hardware store and obtained the appropriate advice and necessary hardware.

Much to her satisfaction, when she put the shelves where she had wanted to so many years ago, not only were they securely placed, but they really pulled the family room together. The finishing touch to the room was putting things on the shelves that had actually come from her grandmother's beautiful apartment. The last item, a photograph of her grandmother as a young girl, made the shelves fully come to life.

She waited in slight trepidation for her husband to remark about her enterprise. She said nothing, and interestingly enough he said nothing either for many weeks, seeming not even to notice them. He finally did comment on them, saying, "Oh, those look nice."

While it still wasn't a perfect marriage, and the shelves had slept much too long under the bed, Deborah was much happier that she had finally begun to meet her needs.

A Positive Activity for You

Think about different situations that you're in where you may need to meet your needs or learn to negotiate for them more successfully. Pick a situation that you probably can handle more effectively than you now are, without having to make a great deal of change in your life.

Perhaps you would like to negotiate more successfully with your husband about which restaurant to go to the next time you go out. Think about some of the ways that you can make clear what your needs are, and what you are willing to give in return if there has to be some compromising or conceding. When it's timely, go ahead and practice being clearer about whatever the situation is that you have chosen to discuss. And don't get discouraged. Remember that learning to speak up clearly and directly on our own behalf takes practice.

Take a moment to think about this gateway before you go on to the next.

Gateway Four: Replenishment - Truly coming home
to our Enchanted Self

Replenishment, joy, pleasure and delight are all parts of truly coming home to our Enchanted Selves. If any gateway is the pivotal gateway for a woman, it is this gateway. This is the gateway that we must return to above all others, as frequently as possible. It is where we fuel up, where we energize. It is where we fill ourselves again so that we can meet the needs of others, be the caretakers of the world, bring up our children, spend time with the elderly, and do the hundreds of womanly tasks that we do, including having a full time job and running a home.

It may seem strange to you at first, but the smartest way to fill up again once we've become depleted is to bring personal satisfaction and replenishment back into our own lives. This means really knowing who you are, loving yourself and knowing how to meet your needs.

If you feel rejuvenated after a great game of tennis, then that works for you. If you try to fill up by going to a comedy performance or having a massage, you may remain on empty if it isn't right for you. Choosing what is right differs from person to person, so invest some good thought into finding out what is right for yourself.

In ***THE ENCHANTED SELF: A Positive Therapy***, I teach how to sort through your memories to get to know yourself, so that you can really tune in on the best forms of replenishment, joy and pleasure for you. A general rule of thumb is to look for what has felt good in the past, and try to either duplicate it or find a way to transform the activity into a form that works for your present stage of life. For example, a long swim in a lake in childhood might now be light swimming, walking in the pool at the local "Y," and a cup of coffee!

Case Vignette

Lisa had been very much a tomboy growing up. Now a mother of five children, she found herself in a maternal role literally 24 hours a day. Often her body ached for climbing trees and for the soccer field.

Lisa shared with me how good she felt and how much personal replenishment she was able to take from a simple activity that developed in a nearby friend's backyard. One of her neighbors had put up a very large trampoline. All the kids would go out and bounce on it, having great fun as they jumped up and down on it.

One day Lisa decided to join them. Before she knew it, she was having the most wonderful time, jumping, bouncing, landing on her bottom and even doing somersaults as she became more confident. This was fabulous! She was moving and jumping, using her great sense of balance and having a wonderful time. Twenty minutes on the trampoline, three times a week, was as close to paradise as Lisa needed to get to during this particular stage of motherhood.

A Positive Activity for You

Think about some of the things you really loved to do when you were a child. You may want to jot some of these down on a piece of paper. They could be activities, hobbies or interests that you had.

Once you have completed your list, take time on and off during the next few days to think about your list. Use your imagination to brainstorm how you could either bring back to life some of your old passions, or refine ways to create new interests that have some of the same features. For example if you loved to roller-skate as a child, you may want to try roller-blading, or you may want to take up ballroom dancing (which may be less risky on the muscles and joints!) Such a treasure hunt for lost joys is an activity that you can do again and again as you search through the story of your life for the very unique factors that can bring you pleasure and rejuvenation again and again.

Take a moment to think about this gateway before you go on to the next.

Gateway Five: Coming Home or Going Away, Finding Tribes in Which to Belong

As women we find ourselves automatically belonging to certain groups. There's the family we're born into, the family we may have created through marriage, and all sorts of other groups going on in our lives: PTA groups, office colleagues and church affiliations, etc.

Many women don't realize how critical it is to belong to groups. Depression feeds very quickly off of isolation. By nature most women not only share commonly in our care taking and in our concerns about others, but we enjoy and thrive when we're a part of the right groups. We want to be connected. We don't want to be isolated.

Choosing the right groups, the right tribes to belong to, is part of the dilemma and the wonderment of going through adult life. While our children don't always have much freedom in choosing what groups they belong to, sometimes they can be so greatly against an activity that we finally let them quit. We may let them leave the Girl Scouts or little league, or perhaps stop taking piano lessons, thus letting them make their own determinations.

But we, as adult women, can on the whole always have the privilege and luxury of picking our groups. It may well be time, as your children get older, to say "goodbye" forever to the PTA. It may be time to find a religious affiliation that is or is not connected to your heritage or what you were initially exposed to.

It may be time to find groups to belong to through technologies that didn't exist ten years ago. I have clients and friends who have found meaningful interest groups through the web. For example, a woman client now belongs to a quilting group that is worldwide. The result is that she not only has gained chat mates, but she has also been able to visit her new friends around the world and been able to act as hostess to many of these friends. As they say, "Who coulda thunk it?"

This is an extraordinary gateway, so take some time getting to know yourself, as you are now, and see the many ways how this can lead you to where you want to connect.

Case Vignette

Selma was brought down emotionally by a developmentally disabled young child and by her sound but somewhat difficult marriage, which included difficult in-laws. She was feeling a bit discouraged and at times even clearly blue. Nothing in her current environment was really picking her up.

Unexpectedly, a girlfriend from her high school days got in touch with her and invited her to join a small group of friends who were going off on a four day woman's-only weekend in New England. When Selma initially approached her husband, he was negative, reminding her of all her household and child responsibilities.

This was exactly what she did not need to hear at the moment. She desperately needed some way to refresh herself in mind, body and spirit. She dug in her heels, made plans to have her child's care covered, and went off with the four women.

Joining this temporary group was extremely beneficial for her. She ended up laughing her way through New England, feeling a sense of connection to people who understood her background and the dreams and hopes she'd had as a teenager. They all shared their own marital dilemmas and were sympathetic to hers. There was even one woman in a somewhat similar situation, with an adolescent who was driving her crazy.

The time flew by, and she returned home feeling uplifted with laughter still tingling in her belly, good food and good times, even physically refreshed from a massage she'd had at the spa. She was certainly good to go for the continued saga of her life. What a wonderful, temporary tribe she'd been part of, and what memories she'd have of their gathering for months to come!

A Positive Activity for You

Try making a list of all the groups you currently belong to. Now divide the list into columns, one column for groups you are happy to be affiliated with, a column for the groups you wish you weren't affiliated with, and a third column for groups that you feel neutral about.

Over the next month or so, take time to brainstorm with yourself in terms of two avenues of adventuring. One is how you might bring more pleasure and happiness into your life by expanding your connection to one of the groups in the first column. At the same time, start to brainstorm a new group, or to look for a replacement for one of the groups in your second column.

For example if you've really had it with a particular women's group you're connected to, perhaps you want to replace that group with something entirely different. It could be a course at the local community college, tennis lessons that you let go for twenty years, a book club or a connection with an old friend. I hope you enjoy this dual process of making your experience even richer with the groups you want to stay connected with, and cleaning house with at least one group that you're ready to get rid of.

Take a moment to think about this gateway before you go on to the next.

Gateway Six: Sharing Our Wisdom, Mentoring and Being Mentored

As women, we live in a golden age. We have more education than women have historically had access to. We live longer; we're healthier; we look better. Everything is really in our favor if we know how to absorb and share our wisdom and knowledge.

The key to making use of all our opportunities, and maybe even the key to a happy and healthy longevity, is learning what we need to learn. What a lot of women don't realize is that mentoring can come in many different forms. I can be sitting with an 85-year-old woman and in listening to the story of her life have my heart warmed and my courage heightened, just by hearing the things she's had to deal with and live through in her many years. I can also be in the presence of a two-year-old and learn the infectious, delightful nature of laughter once more, a lesson I may have forgotten too often. I can be taking a walk at the shore, listening to the sounds of the ocean waves and letting them soothe me, reminding me of the constancy of Mother Nature and her efforts to keep the world whole and in rhythm.

Wherever a woman passes in her life, she can be giving and receiving profound levels of exchange with nature and with other people of all ages and all stages of life. This is indeed what the good life is all about.

Case Vignette

While we were having tea on her back porch, my friend commented, "I'm learning so much from Katie." I said, "Who's Katie?" (I had never heard her talk of Katie before.)

"Katie's that young woman who lives down the street." I said, "Oh! Do you spend much time with her?" She answered, "No actually we never spent anytime together." "Really?" I said. "Yet you're learning from her?" She responded, "Oh yes, though I don't even think she really knows who I am."

Now my curiosity was truly piqued. "Well, how are you learning from her?"

"It's easy. I just watch her house and I watch her. I see how she opens her door and welcomes people, the graciousness and lilt in her voice as she says 'Hello' and 'How are you?' And I watch her sometimes when people are leaving, how she escorts them out, takes them down to their car, or if they're walking she accompanies them partway down the street, her smile radiant and sincere. She may be half my age, but she has a world to teach me around sharing, courtesy, and making people feel truly welcomed."

"Wow," I thought to myself. "I wonder who's around me who has wisdom lessons to teach, someone I'm not even noticing. I'd better go and start looking."

A Positive Activity for You

For a week, take on the personal assignment of intentionally sharing some information, wisdom or part of the story of your own life with someone. Make it your intent to ask for and/or listen for the wisdom, information and ideas around you.

Try to think out of the box. Your information may come from a senior citizen, a very young child, a piece of equipment, a tree or something else in nature. It may also come from something that's been staring you in the face for years, such as a particular cereal box containing information about nutrition, or something equally important that you've stared at a hundred times. You may get a kick out of keeping some sort of log of the incredibly diverse places and people that will bring important new information into your life.

Take a moment to think about this gateway before you go on to the next.

Gateway Seven: Positive Action, Remember the Notion of a Good Deed

This Gateway is the gateway of positive action, or "Why not do a good deed, it can't hurt!"

We're all faced with bouts of discouragement, letdowns and disappointments, and for women, certainly the cycle of life itself has its ups and downs. Anyone fortunate enough to have longevity on her side will inevitably sustain losses and disappointments. None of the Gateways to Enchantment can totally prevent a person from the necessary bumps and grinds of life, but what they do provide are mechanisms not only with which to pick ourselves up heroically, but to strengthen ourselves and make the world a better place for us. One of the very best ways to do this is through positive action. I look at positive action in three ways.

For one thing, it's good practice to take positive action, whether it's about a personal issue in your own life, or to help others. This forces us to practice timeliness, good behaviors, and often good logic and decision-making.

Secondly, taking positive action can definitely help offset loneliness, letdown feelings, and feelings of discouragement. It does this by the act of pushing us into connecting with people, sharing with people and having the opportunity to experience the happiness shared by others when they are affected by something positive that we do. The cliché, "A smile is more infectious than a frown," definitely holds true in this case.

Thirdly, doing positive action helps us to grow emotionally and spiritually. All the great religions of the world and the great thinkers encourage positive action and good deeds as a way of stretching our own capacities as human beings. These effects can be permanent. Think about Helen Keller, a woman who took the steps to positive action, to learn to speak and share her wisdom over a lifetime, even though she herself was profoundly deaf and blind. She not only created a much fuller life and a better world for herself, but she created hope and inspiration for those whom she touched. Even now, many years after her death, her courageous example sends out mentoring lessons of inspiration throughout the world.

Case Vignette

Here is a true story about positive action. Ellen's girlfriend realized that there were many women in their town who really had need for charity and emergency funds. However, some of the women needed help immediately, and going through the process of receiving money from a charity would take long.

Ellen had a wonderful idea. Why not, together with all of her good friends, each put $25 into a "pot." With the start of $250, which she collected, she then gave a "potluck dinner." All her friends came, ate a wonderfully shared meal, and then set about establishing a group, which they called "Womenade."

Periodically, when they heard of a woman who needed help, they helped. They helped one woman buy a suit so she could go on job interviews and finish a job-training program. They helped another pay for extra day care during an illness. They helped others in small and not so small ways.

It was easy. When they started to run low on funds, they had another potluck dinner together, laughed, shared their lives and their ups and downs, and put another $25 each into the pot.

For more information about Womenade, please write to me at DrBarbara@enchantedself.com.

A Positive Activity for You

In the best of all worlds, if you have your full

resources, including health, money, time or whatever else you may need, brainstorm three positive actions that you can take. Whether it involves only you, or whether it would involve the entire world, go for it!

Sometimes this mental exercise is harder than one would think because we are so used to not stretching and just accommodating to our current status that we don't invest much energy into what we would do if we had unlimited resources. After you've done some brainstorming, think in terms of the resources of time, money and energy that you do have, and see if you can create one small step, one positive action, that will move you a little closer to your unlimited goodwill.

For example, if your brainstorming led you to cleaning up the world of all pollution, perhaps you can take one small step by writing a letter to your senator or congressman, suggesting that they fight for clean air standards. Or perhaps you could use your car a little less and walk a little more, or ride your bike.

This would accomplish the extra bonus of good exercise, and make you feel better both physically and mentally.

It's fun to dream. Remember that every dream, with ingenuity and planning, may well become a reality. But in order to become that reality, many steps need to be taken. So take your first, today.

Welcome to the Seven Gateways of Happiness!

May you enjoy every day. Take your time with the Seven Gateways to Happiness. As I mentioned in the beginning, you may decide to work on Getting Your Needs Met and soon discover that to really walk through this Gateway, you have to better recognize your talents and potential. And so you will have to pop back to the first Gateway for a while. That is ok. Don't worry. We work in wonderful circles and spirals as women.

Have courage. As long as you are working on yourself, from the inside out, your will come home, home to your Enchanted Self!

And don't forget to write to me at drbarbara@enchantedself.com I want to know all about your emerging Enchanted Self.

Books by Dr. Barbara Becker Holstein:

The Enchanted Self, A Positive Therapy

Recipes For Enchantment, The Secret Ingredient is YOU!

Delight

Delight
CD-rom version with art, music and voice

Feel Good Stories
Edited by Dr. Holstein and written by her mother,
Bernice Becker

The Truth, I'm Ten, I'm Smart and I Know Everything!
Adult Women's Version of The Truth

Secrets: You Tell Me Yours and I'll Tell You Mine...Maybe

June 2012: *Next Year In Jerusalem*

www.ingramcontent.com/pod-product-compliance
Lightning Source LLC
Chambersburg PA
CBHW071413290526
45789CB00003BA/1387